Contents

Life Before the Light Bulb

Imagine it is the middle of the night and you need to get a glass of water. What would you do? Most likely you would switch on the light. But what if there wasn't a light switch? Imagine there was no electricity or artificial light. This is what it was like for people thousands of years ago. They had to rely on natural sunlight and fire.

Over thousands of years people developed different light sources that led to the electric lights we have today. This is the story of those developments and how they changed human life and civilization.

About 100 thousand years ago, people used firelight to see. First they learned how to keep fire going from a natural source, then how to create it themselves. Gradually they would have got better and better at controlling that fire.

Fire was also very useful for keeping warm, cooking food and keeping people safe. Animals were often afraid of fire, so if people kept a fire going through the night the animals wouldn't attack. The ability to control fire was probably the first step towards human civilization. By spending time together around the fire, people built up a sense of community.

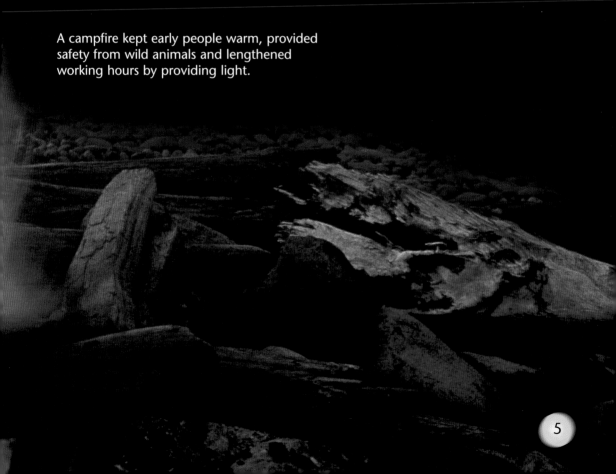

A campfire kept early people warm, provided safety from wild animals and lengthened working hours by providing light.

First Light Sources

Early fires were probably kept in one place. However, soon people discovered how to carry fire. They made torches from sticks or reeds dipped in animal fat. Unfortunately, torches were very dangerous and people got burned. Futhermore, the torches were very heavy and difficult to handle.

About 70,000 years ago people made the first lamps. These were made out of rocks, shells and clay. Stones were hollowed out, and clay was shaped into holders. Then animal fat and straw was added. Straw absorbed the fat and kept the flame glowing. This is similar to how a wick, the string in a candle or an oil lamp, absorbs the wax or oil that keeps a flame burning.

Stones were hollowed out to make crude lamps.

A shell was used as a lamp by adding oil and a wick.

Pottery oil lamps were used in ancient Rome.

Candles

Between 3000 BC and 2000 BC the Egyptians started making torches called rushlights. They soaked the core of a reed in animal fat. Then they would set fire to them. The Romans were the first to weave fibres together and use them as candle wicks.

Ancient candles and lamps primarily used tallow – animal fat – for fuel. This smelled quite bad and made a lot of smoke. By AD 300 the Chinese started making candles from beeswax. Beeswax was a better fuel than tallow because it smelled much sweeter and smoked much less. However, beeswax was expensive, so only rich people could afford to use candles made out of it. It wasn't until the late 1700s that cheaper candles were made with whale oil so poorer people could use them.

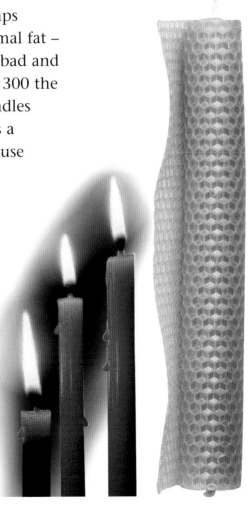

Today most candles are made of paraffin wax (left). Beeswax (right) is also used.

The Search for a Better Light

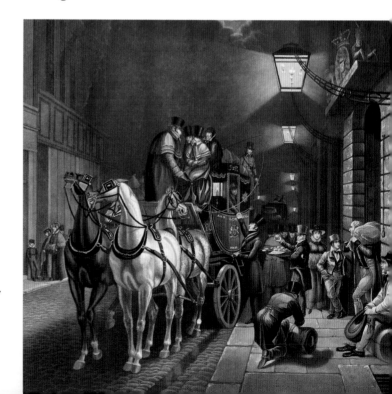

From the 1790s, people started looking for cheaper and better lighting. Fossil fuels, such as petroleum and coal became very popular. In 1792 William Murdock started experimenting with coal gas which was produced by burning coal. At first he used the gas to light lanterns in his home and his company's factory. Then other people started to copy his idea. By 1804 he had become known as the father of the gas industry.

early gas lamp

In 1821 natural gas began to be used. This was found in the ground and didn't need to be made like coal gas. Natural gas was piped from a well into buildings and used for light. Some places, however, did not have natural gas deposits and so could not take advantage of this fuel.

Gas lighting changed the look of London and many other cities.

Early Experiments in Electricity

Electricity is found in many forms. It appears in the sky as powerful lightning bolts. It darts through the human body as nerve impulses. Electric pulses are also used by animals such as the electric ray to stun prey.

As far back as the fifth and sixth centuries BC, people tried to understand electricity. In 600 BC a Greek mathematician called Thales became curious about what is now known as static electricity. He rubbed some wool over a piece of amber and discovered that it attracted feathers, straw and hair.

Over time many more experiments were carried out to learn more about electricity. However, the problem remained that no one knew how to collect and store electricity.

When rubbed, amber acquires static electricity and can attract lightweight objects.

Electric rays use electric pulses to stun their prey.

Electricity: Static vs Current

Static electricity consists of charges that do not move. When someone comes into contact with an object holding static electricity, it is released. On the other hand, current electricity flows through wires. It can be generated in a battery or by a generator powered by steam, oil or other fuels. It is then sent to power such items as radios, televisions and computers.

Collecting Electrical Charges

The Leyden jar, first used in the Netherlands in 1746, was developed by early experimenters to store electric charges.

In the mid-1700s, Dutch scientists worked on ways to collect and store energy. They invented the Leyden jar. This was a glass container with metal foil on the inside and outside. The top of the jar was placed against a machine that generated static electricity which was then collected in the jar. The static electricity remained in the jar until a wire touched the inside and outside foil. If wire touched the foil, then the electricity was released and produced sparks.

Benjamin Franklin noticed the similarities between the tiny sparks of the Leyden jar and the giant sparks made by lightning. He thought they might both be forms of electricity. In 1752 Franklin invented the lightning rod. This metal rod attracted static electricity from a storm cloud. It drew lightning into the ground. This protected buildings and people from being struck by lightning.

A lightning rod draws the charge from a storm cloud and conducts it into the ground instead of a building.

The First Battery

Count Alessandro Volta was also curious about electricity. He wanted to store electric charge and also to produce a steady flow of electricity. In 1800 Volta invented the Voltaic Pile. This device was made of copper and zinc discs and had pasteboard soaked in salt water in between the discs. Volta stacked the discs about 30 centimetres high. At the bottom of the stack was a copper disc. This was a positive terminal. At the top was a zinc disc. This was a negative terminal. The stack was held together by three glass rods. Volta showed that a low current of electricity flowed from the device when a wire was attached to either end. He had made the first chemical battery. He also showed how to produce a continuous electrical current.

Count Alessandro Volta

Voltaic Pile

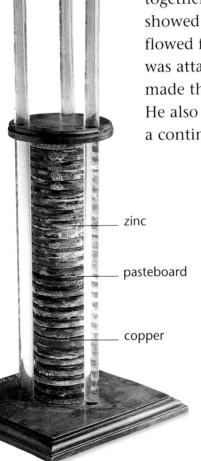

zinc

pasteboard

copper

How a Battery Works

Volta showed that stacking two different metals, each separated only by a moist, porous material, causes a chemical reaction that generates electricity. Today batteries are made with many combinations of elements. Like Volta's pile, they all have negative and positive terminals. The unit of electric potential is the volt, named after the count.

An Arc of Light

Humphry Davy invented the first electric light. In 1809 he connected one wire to the negative terminal of a huge Voltaic Pile and another wire to the positive terminal. Then he placed a charcoal strip between the other ends of the wires. (Charcoal is made mostly of carbon and is created by burning wood or other material.) The charcoal glowed, showing that electric power could be used to produce light. He also passed an electric current through many other materials. When he passed it through a platinum wire, the wire glowed.

Later Davy discovered that if he ran an electric current through two charcoal rods placed slightly apart, a curved band of electric current jumped from one rod to the other. This discovery was called an electric arc. It eventually led to arc lamps, which were first used in a lighthouse in 1862.

This arc lamp dates from the 1870s.

Humphry Davy gave public lectures to demonstrate how the arc lamp worked.

The Light Bulb is Born

Warren de la Rue

In 1820 Warren de la Rue placed a platinum coil in an airless glass tube. He knew that platinum had a very high melting point and believed that it would not melt when an electric current was passed through it. He also thought that if he removed the air from the tube the platinum would not catch fire. Air, after all, is needed for burning. This was the first light bulb. Unfortunately, it was too expensive to be used.

About 20 years later Frederick de Moleyns also created a light bulb which he patented. His light bulb also used an airless glass tube, but de Moleyns placed powdered charcoal between two platinum wires. One problem with de Moleyns' bulb was that the charcoal completely blackened the glass as it burned. This quickly dimmed the light.

What is a Patent?

A patent is legal protection to safeguard a person's ideas and inventions. If someone copies a patented invention without permission, then the inventor may sue or take other legal action. Patents allow people to share their ideas and inventions free from the fear that others might steal them and make money from them.

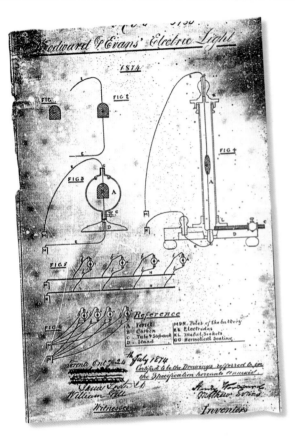

Woodward's and Evans' patent included detailed drawings of their invention.

In 1874 Henry Woodward and Matthew Evans filed a Canadian patent for their version of the light bulb. In 1876 they obtained an American patent on what they now called the electric lamp. To make light, the Canadian team used a threadlike piece of carbon that would glow when an electric current was passed through it. Their glass bulb was filled with nitrogen gas to prevent the carbon strip from burning up.

Unfortunately, Woodward and Evans did not have enough money to perfect their invention. In 1879 Thomas Edison, who had developed similar ideas, purchased the patent from the inventors. With the support of wealthy investors, Edison began the Edison Electric Light Company to further develop his ideas.

Thomas Edison purchased the Canadians' patent and founded the Edison Electric Light Company. This product label shows Edison with his inventions.

The Modern Light Bulb

Joseph Swan demonstrated his light bulb in England in 1878.

Although Thomas Edison is often credited with inventing the light bulb, British scientist Joseph Swan also patented a version of the light bulb. He received his patent in 1878 – ten months before Edison received his. Swan had started work on his bulb in 1860. It had an almost airless tube and a carbon fibre filament. Though his bulb worked, it had a short lifespan, and the light it produced was very dim. These weaknesses were caused by several problems. First the vacuum pumps Swan used did not remove enough air from the bulb. Oxygen caused the filament to burn up quickly. Second the material the filament was made from required a great deal of electrical current to run through it before it became hot and glowed. Finally Swan's power source was a battery which was not strong enough to produce a bright light.

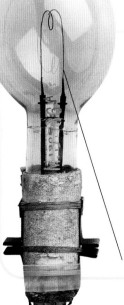

What Is a Filament?

A filament is the material that glows in the centre of a light bulb. Early light bulbs had carbon filaments. Today filaments are made from the metal tungsten which was discovered in 1783. Edison considered using tungsten as a filament in the 1880s, but the brittle metal was hard to work with.

Swan's bulb had a carbon filament.

Most modern bulbs have tungsten filaments.

Edison Improves the Light Bulb

Edison's Menlo Park research team

In the same year that Joseph Swan patented his light bulb, Edison told a *New York Sun* newspaper reporter that he was sure that he could make a light that everybody would use. Even though several kinds of light bulbs had been invented, most homes and streets were still lit by gas because none of the bulbs worked very well. All the previous work on light bulbs, however, gave Edison clues about the approaches his research team should and should not take.

Edison's Invention Factory

Edison's laboratory was stocked with many books, tools and chemicals. Away from the hustle and bustle of nearby New York City, Menlo Park was the perfect place for creative thinking.

The Menlo Park Team

Edison assembled a team of experts to assist him in his laboratory in Menlo Park, New Jersey. From 1878 to 1880 the scientists worked to perfect the light bulb. The hardest part of their job was determining which material worked best as a filament. Edison knew that anything with carbon would eventually burn up, but he wanted to find the substance that would glow the longest.

The Menlo Park team tried thousands of fibres – everything from human hair to fishing line to spider webs. Edison even had samples of vegetable and plant fibres sent to him from around the world. Each fibre had to be made as thin as thread and baked until it was black with carbon. Edison experimented with thousands of materials to determine which would let the bulb glow for an extended period of time.

Edison's team tested many different fibres.

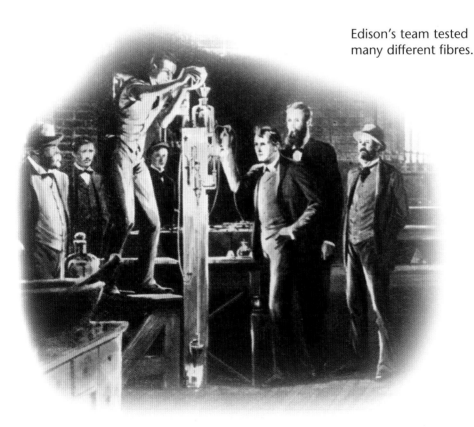

On the Right Track

Edison kept the team working day and night on delicate, painstaking experiments. Finally, in October 1879, they tried a carbonized cotton thread filament that glowed for nearly 15 hours. Edison knew that he was at last on the right track. No other material had glowed nearly as long.

By the end of 1880 Edison and his Menlo Park team had produced a bulb that burned for more than 200 hours. They used Japanese bamboo in a strong vacuum to produce a long-lasting bulb. The team was well on its way to developing the modern light bulb.

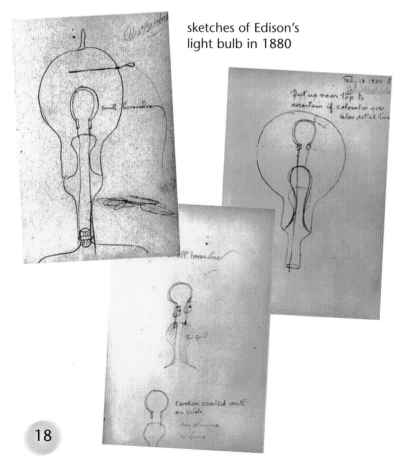

sketches of Edison's light bulb in 1880

Becoming an Inventor

By the time Thomas Edison was 22, he had set up his invention factory and was determined to produce a new invention every ten days. He succeeded. Edison applied for a patent each week and created a major new invention every six months. One invention was the phonograph (shown below) which was an early form of record player. It earned Edison the nickname of the Wizard of Menlo Park.

Perfecting the Pump

Finding a good filament was not the team's only challenge. Many glass bulbs were needed for experiments, so Edison had to employ glassblowers. A filament then had to be carefully inserted into each bulb before the air could be removed and the base sealed.

Although Swan had developed a good vacuum pump in 1878, the pump still left a small amount of air in the bulbs. Edison realized that any air would speed up destruction of the filament. As a result, his team made important improvements to Swan's pump. Eventually they produced a very strong vacuum in each bulb.

This version of Edison's lamp was made in 1880.

Glassblowing

In the late 1800s glass was still made by hand. The glassblower blew air into a hollow metal rod with a glob of red-hot liquid glass on its end. Then the glass was carefully shaped with special tools and cooled until it was hard.

Edison was very famous and was frequently featured in the press.

Spreading the Word

Thomas Edison knew that to sell his light bulbs he had to let people everywhere know about his invention. Most people of the time were not familiar with electric lighting, except for arc lamps. Moreover the dangers of electricity and wires were a little frightening to the public.

Still Edison hoped to make his newly improved light bulb something that people would want to use. On 21st December 1879 he ran the first public notice about the light bulb in the *New York Herald*.

Edison also wanted people to see first-hand what his light bulb could do. On New Year's Eve in 1879 more than 3,000 people came to Menlo Park to see the laboratory illuminated with twenty-five warmly glowing light bulbs. This event was the first of many to present electric lighting to the public.

Before electric lights, every evening at dusk street lighters lit gas lamps that lined city streets.

The SS *Columbia* was the first commercial user of Edison's light bulb.

In 1880 Edison had another opportunity to advertise the light bulb. Henry Villard asked Edison to furnish the new steamship SS *Columbia* with electric lighting. As the ship sailed around South America, people at each port came to see the magically lit boat.

However, Edison faced a setback that same year. Joseph Swan sued him for using his light bulb design which was patented. Swan won the case. Edison then had to make Swan a partner in his British electrical works. The company was renamed the Edison and Swan United Electric Company.

Although Swan received the patent for the light bulb, Edison improved it dramatically. He created a light bulb that was easy to use and affordable.

This sketch was prepared for a sign showing Edison's name in lights.

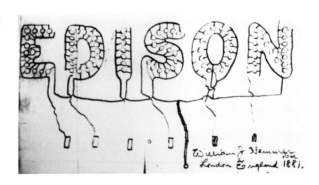

Powering the Light Bulb

The dramatic lighting of the SS *Columbia* was a huge success. It helped to spark the public's interest in lighting. It also allowed Edison to turn his attention to designing electric power sources and ways to deliver power to customers. The electricity for the SS *Columbia* was generated by a single power plant on the bottom floor of the ship. Edison's main interest, however, was to develop central plants that could deliver electricity to widely scattered areas.

early electric meter

Edison started to map out a plan for delivering electricity to everyone. First Edison created a meter to measure electricity usage. People could then be billed for the exact amount of power they used. Second Edison's team used a network of wires to carry the electricity from a central plant to its customers.

electric meter today

reading an electric meter in the 1880s

22

The Edison team worked around the clock, often sleeping only three or four hours each night. They had to create powerful generators to make the electricity. Lighting fixtures, safety switches and fuse boxes were invented. Edison also continued to improve the light bulb itself, looking for longer-lasting and cheaper materials.

As the initial planning drew to a close, Edison decided that a section of Lower Manhattan in New York City called the First District would be a good place to install his first large electric plant. Edison chose New York City because many of his investors were there, and he thought the city would be a good location to show how a delivery system connected to a central plant worked.

the generator for Edison's first electric plant

Pearl Street Power Station began with one generator which produced power for 800 electric light bulbs. Within 14 months, over 12,000 bulbs were aglow. However, with Edison's direct current system, the voltage dropped as distance from the generator increased. Plants had to be built close to users. This was costly and soon led to the development of better systems by rival companies.

23

The Pearl Street Power Station

The power station was a huge task. First a location was chosen for the huge steam generators that would make the electricity. The team decided on Pearl Street in Lower Manhattan. Then wires were laced along telegraph poles, and holes were dug in the city streets for underground cables to deliver the electricity. Finally the First District's buildings themselves were wired.

On 4th September 1882 Edison flipped a switch. For the first time, electric power flowed to the homes and businesses of the First District, setting the neighbourhood aglow with light.

By the end of the 1880s electric lights were being used 24 hours a day, particularly for transport and business needs. Edison had proved that his power and electric lighting system could work on a large scale. He told a newspaper reporter, "I have accomplished all I promised."

model of the Pearl Street Power Station in New York City

Roads in the First District were dug up so that underground cables could be laid down.

Generating Power

A generator converts the energy of motion in the following steps:

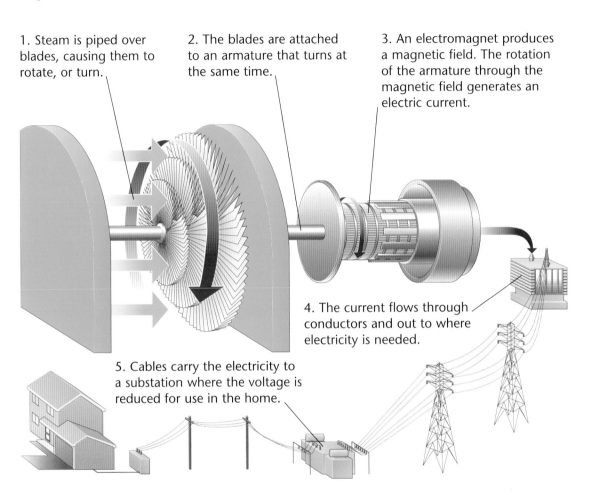

1. Steam is piped over blades, causing them to rotate, or turn.

2. The blades are attached to an armature that turns at the same time.

3. An electromagnet produces a magnetic field. The rotation of the armature through the magnetic field generates an electric current.

4. The current flows through conductors and out to where electricity is needed.

5. Cables carry the electricity to a substation where the voltage is reduced for use in the home.

Portable Generators

Some early generators were small enough to be pulled by horses to the location where a power source was needed. This generator, made by Charles Parsons, was used in England to light up a pond for night skating.

Electricity Changes the World

From 1879 to 1882, 203 customers used Thomas Edison's light bulbs. That number increased to a total of 710 by 1889 and by 1899 had soared to three million customers.

Lights set streets, hospitals, schools and offices aglow. People made changes in the way they lived. After dark they could continue activities that needed light, such as reading and sewing, without eyestrain.

Electricity was soon used for more than just lighting. Electric water pumps and lifts were invented. These innovations made the first skyscrapers possible. In less than twenty years, the electric light and the new electric power industry had changed the world.

Electricity enabled builders to construct huge skyscrapers.

Edison's Death

Thomas Edison died on 18th October 1931, at the age of eighty-four. President Herbert Hoover asked people to dim their lights at ten o'clock that evening in honour of the great inventor.

THE DAILY MIRROR   Monday, October 19, 1931

EDISON, THE WORLD'S GREATEST INVENTOR, DEAD

GENIUS WHOSE DISCOVERIES
TRANSFORMED OUR LIVES

Made Electricity, Moving Pictures and Telephones Realities to All

Thomas Alva Edison, the greatest inventor the world has ever known, died early yesterday at his home in West Orange, New Jersey, U.S.A., aged eighty-four.

Electricity in the Home

In the early 20th century, many different types of electric gadgets, such as those shown below, were invented.

tea maker

electric heater

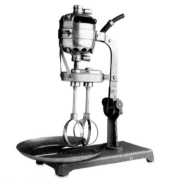

food mixer

People were more willing to invest in electricity when they realized it would allow for many conveniences in addition to lighting. At the end of the 19th century and beginning of the 20th century, all kinds of electric appliances were invented. These included the electric iron, toaster and washing machine.

These inventions made housework easier and life more pleasant. Personal grooming appliances started to appear. Electric heaters and fans were introduced to control temperature. Today new or improved electric appliances for the home are invented every year.

Today we rely on electricity for computers.

Electric Invention	Year Invented
Iron	1882
Fan	1886
Hairdryer	1890
Oven	1891
Toaster	1893
Washing machine	1908
Electric heating	1916

Lighting Today

Since the days of Edison, light fixtures and bulbs have continued to change. In 1910 William Coolidge improved on the General Electric Company's method of making tungsten light bulb filaments. Tungsten has turned out to be the best filament material yet discovered because of its high melting point. With Coolidge's improvements, tungsten became more affordable. Today most light bulbs have tungsten filaments.

Alexandre Edmond Becquerel first created fluorescent bulbs in 1867. Instead of using a filament within a vacuum, an electric current is passed through a gas. Fluorescent bulbs provide as much light as light bulbs, but they use less electricity. Although they were invented in 1867, the bulbs were not introduced to the public until 1938.

Halogen lamps also have a tungsten filament. Halogen in the bulb allows the filament to run at a higher temperature than in a conventional bulb, so the light is brighter.

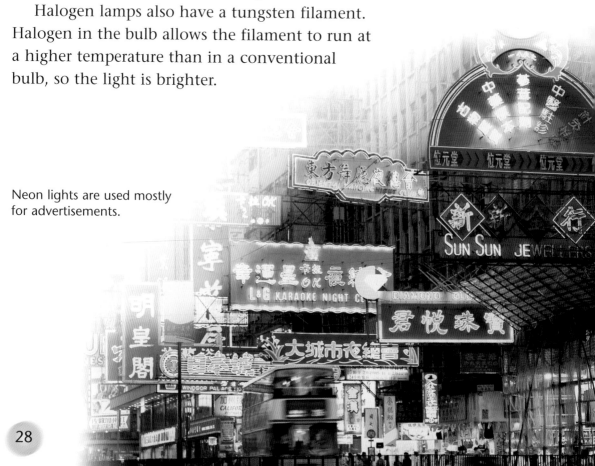

Neon lights are used mostly for advertisements.

Energy and the Environment

Today lighting and appliances produce huge demands for electric power. As a result, great amounts of fossil fuels are burned to generate electricity. Fossil fuels are non-renewable energy sources. Once they are burned, they are hard to replace. Moreover, carbon dioxide gas is released into the air which contributes to global warming.

All over the world, people are trying to develop ways to use wind, water and solar sources instead of fossil fuels, because they are renewable. Hydroelectric dams, for example, use moving water to generate power.

Wind farms generate electricity without damaging the environment.

Solar panels are used to gather sunlight and turn the radiant energy into heat or electric energy. Solar power is a clean and practically limitless energy source. However, it is still costly to use in comparison to coal and oil.

The electricity that hydroelectric dams generate is no different to electricity made from fossil fuels. Yet these dams do not produce the pollution that comes from burning fossil fuels. However, hydroelectric dams present their own threats to the environment by affecting water flow rates and water temperatures.

Hydroelectric dams use water to generate electricity.

From Fire to the Light Bulb: A Timeline

3000 BC and earlier

The Sun, Moon and fire are the main light sources until torches and stone lamps appear.

3000 BC–2000 BC

Wicks and candles are invented.

about 600 BC

The Greek mathematician Thales experiments with static electricity.

1800

Alessandro Volta of Italy creates the first battery, called the Voltaic Pile.

1809

Humphry Davy pioneers arc lighting in London.

1820

Warren de la Rue makes the first light bulb in London.

1874

Henry Woodward and Matthew Evans patent their light bulb in Canada.

1878

● Joseph Swan patents his light bulb.
● Edison Electric Light Company is founded in the United States.

1879

Thomas Edison introduces his light bulb.

Careful planning must be used no matter what kind of power source is developed. When the world finds more ways to use renewable energy sources, the Earth will become a much cleaner and healthier planet.

No one knows exactly what light sources will be used in the future. One thing, however, is certain: people will always want more light in their lives, especially once the Sun has set.

1600s

Improvements are made in oil lamps and candles.

1700s

● William Murdock of Scotland uses coal gas to light his home and his company's factory.
● The Leyden jar is developed in the Netherlands.
● Benjamin Franklin experiments with electricity and invents the lightning rod in the United States.

1823

London streets are illuminated with gas lamps.

1841

Frederick de Moleyns of England receives the first light bulb patent.

1867

Alexandre Edmond Becquerel of France invents the fluorescent light bulb.

1880

Thomas Edison supplies an electric light system for the American ship SS *Columbia*.

1882

Thomas Edison opens the first electric power station in New York City.

1910

William Coolidge improves the tungsten filament, making its production more affordable.

Index